CHRISTMAS MAGIC

Fabulous Festive Designs to Color

BARRON'S

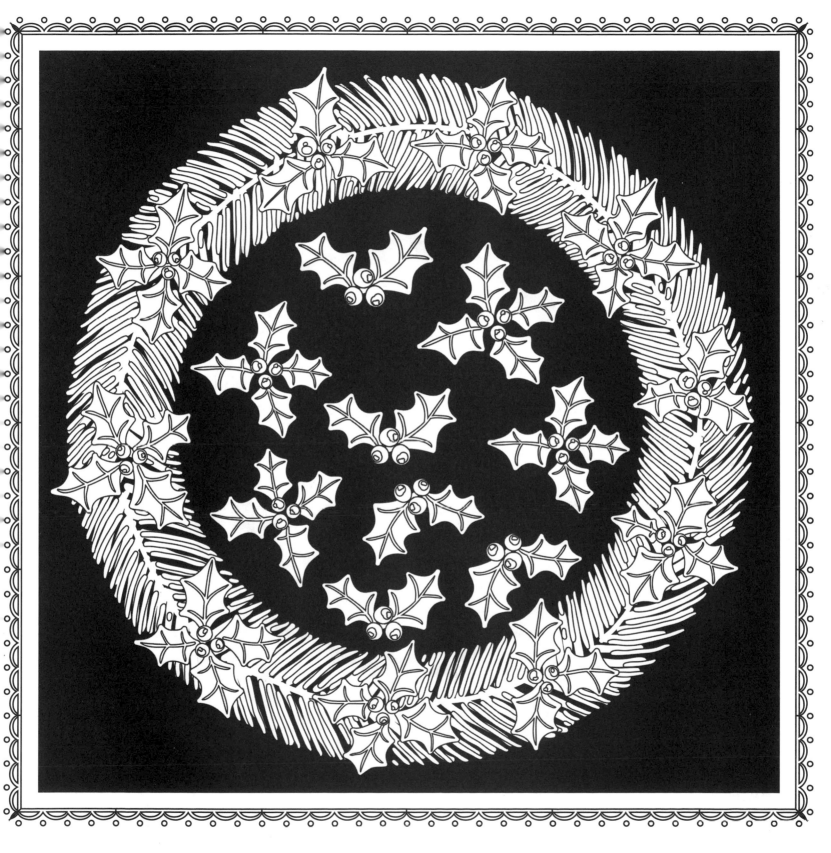

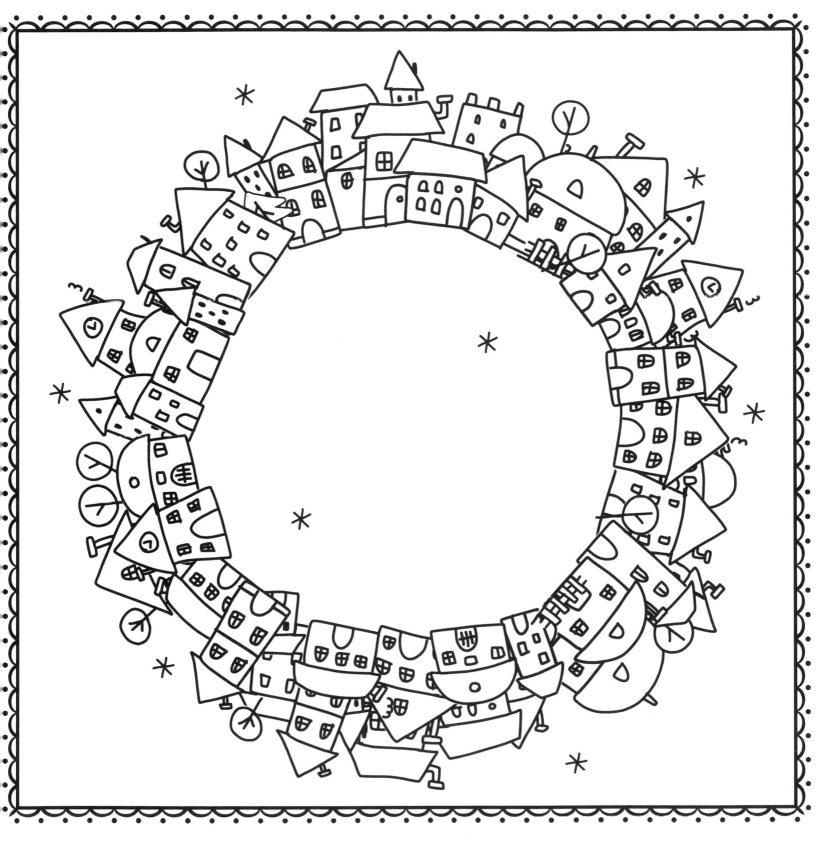

First edition for the United States, its territories
and dependencies, and Canada published in 2015
by Barron's Educational Series, Inc.

Original German title: *Weihnachts—Mandalas:
Wunderbares zum Ausmalen*
© Copyright 2015 arsEdition GmbH, München

All inquiries should be addressed to:
Barron's Educational Series, Inc.
250 Wireless Boulevard
Hauppauge, NY 11788
www.barronseduc.com

ISBN: 978-1-4380-0783-0

Cover design: Grafisches Atelier, arsEdition
Illustrations: Eva Schindler, Atelier für grafische Gestaltung
Picture credits: Getty Images/Thinkstock; Fotolia: cienpiesnf, Coffeechocolates,
lullis, Marina Zlochin, namosh, Olga Drozdova, thingamajiggs

Printed in the United States of America
9 8 7 6 5 4

For best results, colored pencils are recommended.